T0195912

A BIGGER

C

Christ VERSUS Cancer

TERRENCE FEENEY

WESTBOW
PRESS®
A DIVISION OF THOMAS NELSON
& ZONDERVAN

WestBow Press books may be ordered through booksellers or by contacting:

WestBow Press
A Division of Thomas Nelson & Zondervan
1663 Liberty Drive
Bloomington, IN 47403
www.westbowpress.com
844-714-3454

Scripture taken from the New King James Version®. Copyright © 1982 by Thomas Nelson. Used by permission. All rights reserved.

ISBN: 979-8-3850-1495-8 (sc)
ISBN: 979-8-3850-1496-5 (e)

Library of Congress Control Number: 2023923833

Print information available on the last page.

WestBow Press rev. date: 02/21/2024

This is dedicated to the memory of my beloved
aunt, Rev. Frances Malladew Brown.
May 29, 1945–June 7, 2014

My beloved aunt Frances fought a long battle against cancer with a little
c but an even mightier battle for the Lord. The joy of the Lord was her
strength. Christ versus cancer, and she won!

Contents

Acknowledgments

I have had the fortune of being utilized in various areas and categories with topics ranging from domestic violence, drug and alcohol addictions, animal abuse, starvation, school shootings, cancer in all capacities and stages of development, as well as the recovery process, but none more important than his ability to let the words of my mouth and the meditation of my heart magnify his mercy and strength in any situation you face. He has allowed me a platform to show him continuously, "Through it all," as I do that which has been instilled in me with open arms to encourage and esteem my neighbors higher than myself. So shying away from the traditional author pages, my vision is that all readers be lifted up by him and through him so that he alone receives the glory; therefore, cancer, formally known as "the Big C" finally gets introduced to a bigger C and meets its match, which is Christ, and people begin to trust his power, inspiring truth and willingness to save them from every circumstance as his omnipresence and anointing remain unbeaten and incomparable.

You will also witness stories and hear testimonies of people's turnarounds from the seemingly irreversible stage 4 and hospice as his hand journeys through souls of everyday people, patients, physicians and medications they prescribe in the midst of battling through an ailment Christ already atoned for. My hopes and prayers are for healing spiritually, physically, and morally, and that cancer with a little c, is never ever referred to again as the Big C.

Thank you, Jesus, for those times when I failed and was brought to remembrance of your nails.

Thank you for Cecelia Marie Thompson Feeney Bonner, someone who could have easily taken the place of Mary, Jesus's mother, with her obedience, excellence, unconditional love, compassion, and undeniable worship to lift him up and glorify His name.

I would like to acknowledge all the children in pediatric hospitals and those who went on to be with the Lord, all the breast cancer and lung cancer patients, as well as anyone under the sound of my voice who have suffered at the hands of any kind of cancer or know someone who has suffered relentlessly at the hands of this disease, be it hereditary or through personal decisions.

I humbly acknowledge the physicians whose diagnoses can be more than difficult at times to relay and who fight tirelessly to prescribe the accurate medication to accommodate the mercy and grace of God "Through it all."

In addition, I thank everyone worldwide who acknowledge the mercy of Christ versus cancer and eventually turn toward him and seek his grace no matter what you encounter, and receive the salvation that is rightfully yours. My prayers … my acknowledgments.

In 1920, God started our family puzzle, slowly adding pieces over time. He does this for all of us. When he is satisfied with the images he creates in his likeness, he slowly pulls pieces from the puzzle so that the puzzle may be reassembled in heaven. That's what makes heaven so beautiful.

In loving Memory of my Grandmother
Louise Thompson-Blanks
April 17, 1920 – 7/10/2005

Introduction

A Bigger C is about more than cancer;
It's about people's souls and needs.
It illustrates hope through a higher power
When God is incorporated in the disease.

It touches base with sensitive topics
While raising awareness at the same time.
Yet offering comfort as you revisit
A difficult journey in your mind.

We discuss treatments and risk factors,
Screening tests and family history,
Dangers of lifestyle-related choices
From your diagnosis to therapy.

A Bigger C helps you find closure
For those you lose along the way.
And lifting spirits through different scenarios
With the available option to pray.

It presents real-life experiences
That cancer survivors can't ignore.
Issues far less talked about
Than the obvious search for a cure.

A Bigger C takes on cancer
Full circle from the very start,
Finding a balance between prayer and medicine
That God bestowed upon our hearts.

We address not only breast cancer
But every cancerous tumor alive.
And any other malignant growth
That attempts to breed inside.

From stage 0 to hospice care,
We understand the fight is real.
And we won't be discouraged by recurrences.
We still believe Jesus heals.

Be blessed and enjoy!

Christ versus Cancer

Cancer only has one agenda,
And that's to harm at any cost.
While Christ came to seek and save
Those among us who are lost.

Healing was part of His ministry;
He actually raised people from the dead.
Unlike cancer's track record
Of being destructive and likes to spread.

It really doesn't stand a chance
When we look at all the stats.
Christ has power and dominion,
So cancer is overmatched.

He created heaven and earth
Entirely on His own.
And without His outstretched hands,
None of us would have a home.

He remains the reigning champ
And has never lost a fight.
Those souls who suffered from cancer
Still were offered eternal life.

He gave them hope through their storm,
The desire to want to live,
And showed them love and compassion,
Which is more than what cancer did.

Christ prescribes a level of depth
To take you to higher ground;
While cancer thinks nothing of you,
And kicks you when you're down.

At the Cross

There was a list of things purchased
When Jesus laid down His life.
It covered more than just our sins
When He made that sacrifice.

Healing was among those things
That we can rightfully claim.
So I don't know where cancer gets off
Touching homes that are bloodstained.

On His way to the cross,
He knew exactly what to expect.
It's not like cancer is some rare disease
That God hasn't seen yet.

So when He carried that cross,
Breast cancer was already attached.
There were autism and Alzheimer's
That He also included on His back.

He put ovarian and cervical cancers
Where His hands and feet were placed.
His blood washed away colon cancer,
Pancreatic, and prostate.

And He didn't just stop there
When they pierced Him in His side.
He hung for eternal life,
So no one else would have to die.

A lot was accomplished at the cross
And made available to everyone.
So we were delivered from primary cancer,
Breast cancer, and that of the lung.

If I Were President

If I were president of the United States,
I would address how the people feel.
And in the process I would propose
An alternative for them to heal.

I would focus much of my attention
On those who are seriously in need,
And get all the congressional votes
To fight every cancerous disease.

I would tie that beautiful pink ribbon
Around each bill that we legislate
Including the FDA and Oval Office
Until a cure for breast cancer resonates.

I wouldn't raise a penny in state taxes
Unless it was for a medical change.
And insurance that protects all lives
From stage 0 to terminal pain.

I'd make the best treatment affordable
For the indigent and the rich.
With pediatric and breast cancers
At the very top of the list.

I would push to pass a law
That makes screening tests mandatory,
With awareness classes in public schools
And guest speakers telling their stories.

I would uphold the American people
By putting their health first,
Spending less on nuclear missiles
And prioritizing cancer research.

I would certainly acknowledge God
During my term on Capitol Hill,
With talks about that trip to Calvary
That Jesus made to foot our bill.

Woman

Ever notice the location of breast cancer
Is directly above the heart,
The same organ that is required
For your belief in Christ to start?

It's also the area for nursing
Whenever a mother sees fit,
Making a woman more self-conscious
Because of where the cancer sits.

With or without a mastectomy,
Long hair, or shaven head,
Your health is what's important
To prevent cancer from trying to spread.

And don't let *anyone* fool you;
True beauty will always shine.
But society has stereotyped women
And severely crossed the line.

You will remain a phenomenal woman,
A sculpture of the begotten Son.
And this is just another obstacle
That you are empowered to overcome.

You are accomplished and the epitome of courage.
And breast cancer knows it too.
That's why God designed all human life
To miraculously come through you.

Natural woman, let's hear you roar,
Shoulders back with one less rib.
Because in my bold opinion,
You're the strongest creature to ever live.

5

Know Your Options

Breast cancer affects everyone
In spite of gender or race.
And awareness is imperative
To prevent a costly wait.

Self-examinations are important
As you become more informed.
Early detection is the best way
Of considering yourself warned.

There are mammograms and biopsies
That are available for us too.
Doctor appointments and checkups
If you are uncertain of what to do.

Even if you are diagnosed
With a form of breast cancer,
There are options and treatments
And support groups to provide answers.

Radiation and chemotherapy
Are more commonly seen.
A mastectomy could be a preventive method
If you discover you have the gene.

You are more than a conqueror.
Regardless the outcome of an x-ray,
"Strong, resilient, and determined,"
Are what the results should say.

Thousands of women have overcome;
Trust me, you are not alone.
There are cancer survivors nationwide,
A testament we stand by our own.

Remember, you have options.
Research and think it through.
Examine your breasts, consult a physician,
And do what's best for you.

If cancer affects one, it affects us all.

(Dedicated to the Rev. Frances Malladew Brown.)

Recurrence

When cancer goes into remission,
The last thing anyone expects to hear
Is that the mammogram shows signs
That the cancer has reappeared.

A recurrence of breast cancer
Is not foreign to the medical field.
There have been cases prior to yours
That women faced and didn't yield.

You may feel that it's a setback
After everything you did.
But you have to be just as relentless
As this breast cancer is.

There are still treatments available,
And various options like the first time.
With experienced doctors to walk you through,
Showing compassion to ease your mind.

So don't get down on yourself;
Your life is nowhere near the end.
It just means you get a second chance
To kick cancer's butt again.

You'll bounce back inevitably
Because you have been through this before.
So cancer should be the one scared
Of the fight that it's in for!

The greatest recurrence of all
Was the resurrection of Christ.
And unlike the intentions of cancer,
He came to give us eternal life.

No Return

My prayers come by faith
And attached to a special request.
They apply to *all* forms of cancer,
Not just ovarian and breast.

I pray with all my heart
For total recovery to take place,
And bodies to be free of cancer
With not one single trace.

My wish is that this disease
Be sent back to the pits of hell.
And during our race for a cure,
We find salvation as well.

I'm trusting that one day
A final healing will break through.
And this malignant tumor
Won't have a body to return to.

There will be absolutely no chance
To battle into position
Because the power of God in medicine
Will keep cancer in remission.

We'll see more evidence of our rallies,
Donations, and all our prayers
The day that we wake up,
And cancer is no longer there.

Inside Out

God, cancer and medicine
Have two things that three share
Yet when God is in the equation
It doesn't matter who else is there.

The first thing is they start on the inside
Having something to do with pain
And the second is they all have the ability
To produce some kind of change.

Medicine for cancer won't always help
Whatever it is you are going through
And while God is busy working on them
They can't change the God in you.

Your inside is like an incubator
The ideal temperature for any disease
But prayer is still the antidote
To help you function if you believe.

If it is visible on the outside
That breast cancer has taken its toll
And the surgery and different treatments
Have more side effects than you were told.

Then you just reach a little deeper
Beyond the realm of such
A location that cancer can never go
And watch God shape things up.

In order for medication to be responsive
And the process of healing to begin
Salvation is still that membership
And faith is what lets God in.

Believe It or Not

Believe it or not, there are millions
Who are looking for a cure,
From preachers to prisoners, senators to kids,
Mothers to the couple next door.

Believe it or not, science and medicine
Have come a mighty long way,
And we also see results
When we bond together and pray.

Believe it or not, we're closer today
To bringing cancer to its knees
Than at any other time
That we've battled this disease.

Believe it or not, early detection
Has been responsible for saving lives,
And different foods have been linked
To help prevention through us inside.

And believe it or not, not all cancer
Is hereditary with a rapid pace,
And some people who tested positive
Later miraculously showed no trace.

Believe it or not, we still believe,
And that's the positive on which we stand.
Because believe it or not, there's no disease
That's impossible in God's hands.

The Miracle in Medicine

If I sit back and say nothing
While miracles are being performed,
Or let myself receive all the credit
For people making it through the storm,

Then I wouldn't be any different
Than the attacks that cancer makes
If I miss golden opportunities
To paint a picture of Jesus's face.

It does a disservice to cancer patients
When they are battling the disease,
And we don't lead them to salvation,
The true foundation for their needs.

I'm thankful for the progress in medicine
Through some of our greatest minds.
But imagine if we teamed up with God,
How many cures we would really find!

The miracle we look for in medicine
Won't do away with emotional scars.
That kind of miracle can't be found
In a pill, capsule, or jar.

When research does not include God,
It changes the success rate.
Then all of a sudden, the medical field
Has more complications to face.

Please make no mistake about it;
God does still provide.
But some healing involves our decisions
As this nation attempts to rise.

Beyond You

It's been said for many years
That things happen for a reason,
And there's a time and place for everything
In and out of season.

What if there is a lesson behind cancer,
And the real focus for this disease
Is a big part of a humbling experience
To distract us from our own needs?

Maybe God allows certain sicknesses
To go on the way they do.
So the extension of His character
Can put the final touches on you.

What if your battle with breast cancer
Was designed to be a beacon of hope,
Another instrument of sheer resilience
For others to learn how to cope?

Could you handle the responsibility
Of looking past your own pain
And lay it all down on the line
To preface someone else's change?

Are you willing to be proactive
And raise awareness throughout your life,
Inspire others with encouraging deeds
While still giving honor to Christ?

Jesus suffered with no medication,
Carrying that heavy cross on his back,
And He made the world's biggest sacrifice.
But how often do you think about that?

No Match

There is absolutely no chance
That cancer is more powerful than Christ.
And *no* treatment can produce the miracles
That He's performed in your life.

God doesn't need any medicine
To set breast cancer free,
Or to stop a malignant tumor
From spreading so rapidly.

He can heal without treatment
And deliver hope for every pain.
He died to save more lives
Than cancer has ever claimed.

That cross was our life support;
It accomplished more than anyone did.
And the empty tomb was further proof
That Jesus does still live.

There is a clean-cut difference
From the blood that He shed
Versus the abnormal cells from cancer
That disastrously spread.

He has prepared a place for you
That no diseases can enter.
So breast cancer can only exist
On earth or a treatment center.

So if you're seeking more signs,
A prophetic word, or revelation,
God is still the omnipotent,
And the lord over your medication.

Stage 4

Stage 4 cancers are metastatic,
Which means it traveled beyond the breast
And no longer in the regional lymph nodes,
Like the other stages it left.

The prognosis at this point
Is extremely difficult to treat.
But it doesn't mean this disease
Is too far out of God's reach.

Stage 4 is said to be terminal,
Forming the extremity where it's at.
Final and not medically feasible
For any chance of it turning back.

Any time a condition is stage 4,
Severe enough for hospice care,
It opens another door for Christ
To show you He is still there.

He was present during the screening
And before the diagnosis was made.
He is the same God when it's precancerous
As He is in the fourth stage.

Don't underestimate the power of self-examinations
Because early detection shouldn't be ignored.
Many women didn't utilize this method
And could have possibly avoided stage 4.

Breast cancer awareness has risen,
Yet so has the Son of Man.
And stage 4 was already cured
Like He closed the hole in His hand.

Stage 4: God can do anything but fail.
Don't count Him out!

No Circumstance

I'm sure it's difficult battling cancer
If your health is falling apart,
And doubt adds its two cents
To shatter what's left of your heart.

But before you make a declaration
That gives tribulation the crown,
Or decide you can't win for losing
Because your circumstances got you down ...

Let me tell you something about cancer
That you may not want to believe
Because when it comes to certain stages,
You think your outcome is preconceived.

Cancer has never had the authority
To claim anything over your life.
It can't determine how your story ends;
That's established by you through Christ.

You say you can't turn the corner
Because this time your hands are tied.
And no treatment seems to be working
That any doctor has prescribed.

God knows about your predicament,
And his grace is more than enough.
He'll cover all your shortcomings
And breast cancer no matter what.

No circumstance can ever explain
Some of the miracles I see.
His deliverance and power to heal
Are simply beyond me.

It Is Finished

A lot of diseases can be misleading
And never imply hope.
They always give us the impression
That there's no way we can cope.

But I happen to know a thing or two
That proves this theory wrong.
So you don't have to feel defeated
As if you can't go on.

Diseases like cancer have one purpose,
And it's deeper than destroying life.
It's really to try and undo
What was already done by Christ.

See, the enemy is not a fool.
He knows Jesus has our backs.
So he uses breast and thyroid cancers
To lead one of his many attacks.

He'll even throw in neuroblastoma and bone cancer.
But the promise of God is ensured,
So pancreatic, lymphoma, and prostate
Fall under His ability to cure.

Your healing was already established
Through the blood and power of grace.
So don't let ovarian or cervical cancers
Cause your belief to deteriorate.

Jesus prepared a place for you,
So why not give Him a try.
Step out and take what's yours,
And kiss cancer goodbye.

When He said, "It is finished,"
He didn't exclude a certain disease.
God meant exactly what He said
Because He provided all that you'll need.

No Matter What It Looks Like

I'm sure you've heard the saying,
"All that glitters is not gold,"
And how cancer doesn't discriminate;
It attacks both young and old.

Well I'd like to add a few more
To take with you along the way
Because *no* disease that ever existed
Is more powerful than what God has to say.

He was wounded for our transgressions,
And cancer is not exempt.
He was bruised for our iniquities,
So we were healed is what He meant.

The role of any disease
Is to first shake us up inside.
And fill our spirits and minds
With thoughts of not wanting to die.

But no matter what it looks like,
There's a silver lining somewhere.
And maybe you can't see it now
Because of your latest medical scare.

But let me assure you
That cancer in *every* stage
Loses some of its momentum
When we lift our voices in praise.

So don't let it silence you,
And never give up the fight.
Cancer or no cancer,
No matter what it looks like.

Check It Out

Breast cancer has some risk factors,
Just like every other disease.
There is family history or symptoms
With the awareness we all need.

Genetics make up 5 to 10 percent,
Yet it's still a factor nonetheless.
And there's age and just being a woman
That qualifies you to get checked.

You can reduce the risks
By taking care of yourself,
Taking vitamins and eating vegetables,
And monitoring your health.

And avoid a lot of radiation exposure.
And exercise every day;
It will give you a better chance
If cancer does come your way.

Some early symptoms are swelling
Or thickening of the breast skin.
Some dimpling or change in the nipple
Is also likely to begin.

Take notice of any lumps,
And get an opinion if there's breast pain,
Leaking fluids other than milk,
A lactation history, or sudden change.

So self-exams are very important.
It's the hand-and-eye test
Because no one knows better than you
Any discomfort in your breast.

There may not always be a red flag,
Which is clearly the reason why
Screening is also very important,
And for women, strongly advised.

In Exchange

So much has been given up
To try and make this disease stop.
Doctors and nurses work tirelessly
In treatment centers around the clock.

And if we could offset some of the hurt
That has generated over the years,
Compensate all of the families,
And roll back the river of tears,

It would be worth the exchange.
In place of those heavy hearts
To chip in with science and medicine
And screening tests before it starts.

Any time spent raising awareness
To possibly save another life
Puts restrictions on cancers' advances
When we make that sacrifice.

Whether I'm involved with pediatrics or adults,
I don't have the right to choose.
After all the pain in my life
And barriers that God has removed.

We owe it to ourselves and others
To fight breast cancer and prostate
Colorectal, ovarian, and Hodgkin's,
And the breath that lung cancer takes.

In exchange for a little kindness,
You can change a child's tone
Who has been battling leukemia all their life
In a children's hospital more than home.

One person can *always* make a difference
As long as you're willing to try.
It was one who laid down His life,
So none of us had to die.

The Good News

Many newspapers clips and articles
Are reminiscing about singing the blues.
And far too often, just like television
They don't tell you the good news.

They don't always let you in
On what the latest research is.
Or the results from a lab testing
That the government recently did.

But the good news is that the gospel
Was here before cancer was.
And healing was part of the ministry
That Jesus displayed under God's love.

No one had any access
To modern-day medicine.
They stood on the promises of God
And the power that faith transcends.

The good news is in spite of cancer,
God has opened so many doors.
And it's given doctors amazing opportunities
And the ability to find cures.

The good news when it comes to cancer
Is you don't have to live in fear.
There's redemption through Jesus and plenty of hope
That we've been spreading for years.

There are miracles in medicine
That are still taking place.
And the good news for you
Is you no longer have to wait.

So whatever your sickness is,
Don't lose sight of what you believe.
The good news is still *salvation*
Above every religion and disease.

Right Where You Are

The most peculiar thing about diseases
Is that regardless of how they start
No one is ever exempt,
And location plays no part.

You can have a perfect bill of health
With a house somewhere in the hills,
And have a void so huge inside
That no amount of money can fill.

Whether you're on top of the world
Or in a mansion with a fancy suite,
Born in the ghetto or in the suburbs,
A celebrity or someone discrete.

You can also be in your private jet,
Across the ocean traveling afar,
And still be diagnosed with cancer
No matter where you are.

And right where you are today,
God can turn your life around,
Removing all cancerous tumors
And anything else the doctors found.

He'll revisit those dark places
That are causing your thoughts of suicide,
And break that spirit of disbelief
In every treatment to make cancer die.

Hospital bed or a waterbed,
God will meet you right there.
He just needs a point of contact
And the actual faith in your prayer.

Salvation can still be yours.
Don't let cancer cause you to quit.
God's not intimidated by any disease.
He'll show up right where it is.

Who Did You Expect?

While no cancer diagnosis
Is exactly music to the ears,
Breast and ovarian for women
Are particularly devastating to hear.

And as shocking as the news is,
What really comes as a surprise
Is when God shows his face
Before chemo is even applied.

Or when you go for that second opinion
To confirm whether cancer is there,
And you're thanking God all the way home
For answering yet another prayer.

Who did you really expect
When you called upon his name,
And the screening test was still positive
As your blood work showed the same.

When the results from the operation
Said all the cancer was not removed,
Did you then decide to turn to God
Because you had nothing else to lose?

If those of you being evil
Can give good gifts to men,
How much more will your heavenly Father
Let his power of healing extend?

Survivors

Women and men have fought diseases
Ever since the beginning of time,
Through some of the toughest illnesses
That attacked both body and mind.

They have defeated some incredible odds
When not even doctors thought they would survive,
And when all the cards were stacked against them,
Anticipating that they would die.

Through treatments and constant pain,
These same women and men
Refused to accept the idea
That cancer would get the best of them.

While undergoing chemotherapy,
Some women may have lost their hair
But never lose their wills to live,
And battle back from intensive care.

They made a liar out of the devil
In more ways than one.
Not only did they beat cancer,
But they told everyone what God has done.

The beauty of being a survivor
Is other people can turn to you,
Knowing you are more than a conqueror,
And it's something you have been through.

So there is a level of responsibility
That each survivor will get.
Raising awareness is an amazing mission,
But the battle for some is not over yet.

Family History

A team of experts use advanced treatments
To fight the many forms of breast cancer,
Including metastases and recurrent diseases,
As we seek new and improved answers.

Most women with breast cancer
Will never know where it came from
And cannot pinpoint the exact cause,
Even with all the research done.

And when it comes to family history,
There's a cycle that genetics play
And studies that there's always evidence
Of damage to cells' DNA.

While family history can't be avoided,
There are medical decisions you can make.
Routine checkups and screening tests
Are conscious steps you can take.

Now things like smoking and drinking
Can certainly compound your risks.
But you are more likely to develop cancer
With a family history in the mix.

It's increased 5 to 10 percent
If you're someone who has the gene.
But it's no guarantee you'll get cancer
As challenging as it may seem.

Many women who have risk factors
Live a full life just fine.
And in spite of having a family history,
They never show precancerous signs.

You're also a part of another family,
Regardless of any disease.
And that history connects you to Christ
Through the power of Abraham's seed.

A Bigger C

Cancer is often referred to
As that dreaded C word.
With its progressive and rapid movements,
It should be considered a verb.

But since I know a bigger C
That can spread just as fast,
It's impossible not to give Him a chance
When I know His medical past.

He healed and reversed the diagnosis
Of cancer in stage 4.
He stepped in and took over
When physicians could do no more.

He was behind stem cell research
And bone marrow surgeries.
He is bigger than radiation treatment
And chemotherapy.

Christ is that bigger C,
And He knows what you're going through.
He can also turn your situation around
Before you know what hit you.

Cancer is trying to claim the lives
Of those God has put here,
Tormenting their bodies and minds,
Causing people to live in fear.

But if you'll just believe
And let salvation play a part,
You'll see how powerless cancer is
When Christ is in your heart.

Everywhere You Look

There are two things about fighting breast cancer
That it really has in its favor.
One is the huge awareness foundation,
And two is that God is our Savior.

From television shows to the internet,
There is support all over the place.
Commercials, local stores, and churches
All display some form of faith.

Sporting events and best sellers
Join in against this fight.
Movies and poetry support fighting breast cancer
In this hard-fought battle in life.

Songwriters, billboards, and producers
Raise awareness in their own way.
While preachers in robes uphold the ribbons
Each time we kneel and pray.

Communities and women's support groups
Understand the battle is not over.
We have documentaries and live testimonials
With awareness month in October.

Everywhere you decide to go,
And everywhere you look,
There are reminders of strong survivors
And the lives that cancers took.

We use them to build hope
And inspire those like me and you.
So you'll see you are *never* alone
And the progress we're making too.

That's why everywhere you look
There are signs and murals so no one forgets,
And so this generation leaves its footprints
For the generations after the next.

All the While

Remember when you were first diagnosed,
And how you thought your world would end,
And you really just wanted to be alone
Away from family and friends?

You didn't know whether to yell or cry,
Blame God himself or pray.
And telling someone was out of the question
When you couldn't find the words to say.

But while you were yet grieving,
What you failed to realize
Was that your reaction to the situation
Came to God as no surprise.

Long before your hospital visits,
He was working on your behalf.
Before you even knew what chemo was,
Or any of the options you had.

And when cancer had you up all night,
With your body rejecting the medication,
God was already in the midst
Of scheduling your emergency operation.

And while you were busy making plans,
In case you didn't pull through,
Trying to secure your children's future,
God had that figured out too.

What you probably didn't know
Is that every disease we face
Is just another opportunity
For us to walk by faith.

And all the while God's vision
Was much bigger than mine and yours.
So while medical research panics,
He's healing hearts that are unpure.

The Wait Is Over

Every procedure has a process
That requires some extra time.
Whether it's treatment for breast cancer
Or a research we're trying to find.

The delay may be an actual cure
That we all have been waiting on.
Or the results from your blood work
That sometimes seem too long.

Whether you had cancer removed
And you're waiting for the outcome,
Or really hoping it doesn't return
Long after the surgery is done.

It could be a kidney match
That is causing you to wait.
Or even after the operation
To see if the kidney will take.

But when the joy of the Lord
Is your strength and life,
Then your wait won't be as excruciating
As the battle of a cancer fight.

There won't be multiple setbacks
When a sinner's conversion is made.
You'll undergo one transformation
For your life to be blessed and saved.

Peace doesn't have to be put off
Or based on how you feel.
God's sovereignty is awesome,
And so is His power to heal.

One More Year

Everyone's time on earth is precious.
As each year swiftly fades away,
And tomorrow comes so fast
That it often feels like yesterday.

And for someone with terminal cancer,
Who only wants the progression to stop,
It can be more difficult for them
To not constantly watch the clock.

What harm would it have done
To have you around one more year
After all the lives you personally changed
And affected while you were here?

Just one more Christmas to celebrate Jesus
While cancer was on your back.
Showing the world resilience and hope
When a disease is on the attack.

It would have given you another chance
To let people see His amazing grace
And tie up some loose ends.
And say, "I love you," face-to-face.

I thought out of all people
God would have kept you around
At least for one more year
While a cure was being found.

One more year to be with your children
And grandkids alike
Was one less year of suffering
To be in the presence of Christ.

(In loving memory of Rev. Frances Malladew Brown.)

Christ in the Cure

I want a cure for cancer
As bad as the next person does.
But I also want an available treatment
That offers people eternal love.

My hope is that during the suffering
Some kind of humility is reached.
And a better person comes out of it
With a lifestyle and power to teach.

Somewhere along this cancer journey,
Instead of Christ getting the blame,
I want every nation to rebuke this curse
And call out Jesus's name.

You'll find solace and tranquility
The moment you look to Him.
It will ignite His healing power
And strengthen all medicine.

Christ is your turnaround
For everything you want and more.
He's the remedy for *all* your problems
And the solution they need for cures.

Cancer has a lot of followers
Who've made fear a part of their life.
And when your trust is more in man
It excludes the hands of Christ.

You don't have to look very far
To see the reflection of His face.
He has healed you on numerous occasions,
And that then was His grace.

We all want to be made whole,
From our toes to the top of our head.
But what good is physical health
If your soul is still dead.

Someday

Someday, within a matter of time,
I'm sure we'll see each other again.
And we'll talk and do some catching up,
Just like a couple of old friends.

It was such a bitter separation
That lung cancer and emphysema maliciously caused.
And it left me a little upset with God
For not just removing it all.

So now I keep telling myself
That although a cure never came,
There were other aspects of healing
That God used for my change.

Someday when my run is over,
We'll look down, side by side,
And watch over some others with cancer
Who actually did survive.

We'll surely get another chance
To discuss what the eagles did,
Or how great you were at bowling,
And the first bike you bought me as a kid.

I can still hear those Bible scriptures
That you memorized by heart.
And how the anointing impacted our conversations
So we were never really apart.

Someday the legacy you left behind
Will continue leading souls to Christ.
And they'll distinctly hear your voice
Through every poem I write.

(Dedicated to Keith W. Feeney, Sr., 1947–2016.)

Little Did You Know

When the doctor read the medical report
On the diagnosis concerning your health
There was something he declined to tell you
Or perhaps didn't know himself.

He failed to mention some important details
That could not only have saved your life
But could also lead others with cancer
To a healing found in Christ.

He never thought to remind you
That once the prognosis is out of his hands
There is not much more he can prescribe
With there being limitations to man.

See little did you know
While you were consumed by medicine
God was also working on the inside
So your soul would never end.

For some it may come as a surprise
That cancer vanishes without a trace
Because little did you know
You were already saved my grace.

And little did you know
That before you were born
God had it all figured out
How you would handle this storm.

All throughout your life
God has spared you the same way
As he kept you so many times
Even when you refused to pray.

Cancer

Cancer, you have caused enough problems,
Terrorized people and shattered dreams,
Poisoned minds and blocked paths,
All while tearing families apart at the seams.

You've shipwrecked some of the strongest people
Who went on to be with the Lord
As they fought with the full armor of God,
Shield of faith and sword.

You used all forms of sick tactics
To spread your disease around,
Attacking wherever you possibly could
To bring our spirits down.

You attempted to create division
When you took away some of our kids,
Harassing their tiny immune systems
Before they barely had a chance to live.

But we're not afraid of you.
No matter who you try to exploit,
We bounce back in unity
So the whole world can hear our voice.

And we will eventually find a cure
That will track you down *anywhere*,
From nursing homes to children's hospitals
Because we know you're hiding there.

Whether it's breast cancer or pancreatic,
Cervical, colon, lung,
Ovarian, or any primary cancer,
We will fight you until our change comes.

Guess Who?

There's been an ongoing debate
That's talked about everyday.
Some of us saw it in our own lives
As well as in others along the way.

And each day there's more development
That consistently supports this claim.
It's not a figment of our imagination
Or a myth subject to change.

For years we read documents,
Bible scriptures, and stories of Christ,
So we heard all about the healings
And how people came back to life.

We saw breast cancer survivors
Overcome some amazing things,
And people walk out of hospitals
On the strength of incredible wings.

Shocking looks on doctors' faces
Give the medical field a scare
When there are follow-up visits by patients,
And cancer is no longer there.

There have been reported counts
Where the blind have recovered their sight.
And ten men were delivered from skin disease,
Which was cancer in their day and life.

And the number of miracles is going up
As sources have revealed.
And it surely can't be an accident
That so many are getting healed.

I Have Had It

Cancer, the heartaches that you caused
Have been heavy on my mind
And I know there's more then one of you
With various stages in each kind.

I am far beyond devastated
Over the amount of lives you took
So I won't be displaying compassion
Or beating around the bush.

I don't know anyone else's tolerance
Or the point before they break
But I resent you so much
That I have to set the record straight.

I dislike your positive diagnoses
And how you keep dodging a cure
I hate what you represent
And the devil you're working for.

I am especially crushed
When it's children you go after
Whose memories and tender voices
We can still hear in the distant laughter.

And whether you know it or not
Some of those people were my family and friends
And I can't stand those recurrences
When you pop back up again.

You took away pastors and world leaders
Mothers and fathers from their kids
And left us with the responsibility
Of explaining to them what you did.

I despise the thought of you
And resent each act of sin
And bind every curse you carried out
So it never prospers again.

Cancer I know your main goal
Was to make people live in fear
And turn their backs on God
But we know that he still hears.

And that was my childhood buddy
That you ripped right out our hands
And one amazing human being
To the world he was known as "MAN"

(Dedicated to: Cedric Holmes - RIP)

Only God Knows

No one understands everything
That God allows to take place.
Or how long diseases and illnesses
Will go on and test our faith.

And you're probably wondering yourself
What the story line is of your pain.
And by you suffering from cancer personally,
What does anyone have to gain?

And is makes perfectly good sense
To ask God, why you?
And to seek answers for breast cancer
After all you have gone through.

I blamed doctors and medicine
When those I loved were called home.
And I even questioned God myself;
So trust me, you are not alone.

And I still don't have a clue
Why the merciful get treated like that.
I thought they would be the last ones
That cancer would have under attack.

But the one thing I do know,
Because I was fortunate to see it before,
Is that the proof of God's existence
Outweighs the absence of a cure.

You Are Not Your Disease

Two things really stand out
In the society in which we live.
One is the effect of labels,
And two is the unwillingness to forgive.

We also have the tendency
Of calling out people's names,
And identifying who they are
With the severity of their pain.

We are quick to associate
What a person is going through
With the complications of their illnesses
Or what they might respond to.

But you are *not* ovarian,
Lung, or breast cancer.
No one ever called you, "Tumor."
And Jesus is still the answer.

Cancer is not your description,
And it doesn't make up a person's heart.
The qualities that define you
Are what really set you apart.

Going up against any disease
Can speak to your character at times.
But it doesn't make you that disease,
Though it tries to pick your mind.

No matter how bad it hurts,
This here is your life.
Cancer wants to take over your body,
But you still have plenty of rights.

Not on My Watch

Coming to anyone's defense,
Never a picture in the devil's eyes
And certainly not when it comes to cancer;
He would much rather see you die.

If he can't affect you mentally,
He'll attack through insurance costs.
And then drive a nail in your spirit,
And try to finish you off.

But I can't just stand by,
Grow weary, or walk away
When I know one of your treatment options
Is still available if you pray.

If somehow the true message of healing
Gets incorporated in everyone's life,
Then suddenly all forms of cancer
Would meet its match in Jesus Christ.

People would become more conscious
Of any risk factors they face,
When their awareness and decisions
About breast cancer are led by faith.

You would no longer get the impression
That you were at the end of your rope.
Because the effectiveness of prayer
Gives all cancer patients hope.

And it gives everyone eternal life
Once you accept what Jesus did.
You'll experience a new therapy
Through that relentless mercy of His.

So I had to let you know,
In case one day you need a friend,
You'll find one in His Word,
The real miracle in medicine.

Not the End of the World

While certain topics are a bit sensitive,
This conversation is long overdue.
Because all everyone seems to think about
Is what they're financially going through.

But when it comes to terminal illnesses,
Any sickness, or failing health,
You'll be surprised at just how much
The Word of God can offer help.

Diseases have always historically
Taken our eyes off the prize,
Forgetting that once we pass away,
The dead in Christ shall rise.

It is appointed once for every man
To take his final breath,
But you don't have to lose your soul
On this journey in the process.

Cancer is *not* your God.
Nor should we live in fear.
No one knows the coming of the Lord,
So make a difference while you're here.

It is typically a normal reaction
To question the unknown,
Or when you have to adjust to change
With the outcome not clearly shown.

But dying is not the worst thing
That can actually happen in life.
You can live well beyond one hundred
And never get to experience Christ.

So look at it from this perspective:
You will get to see Jesus first.
And from what I've heard about heaven,
It is a lot better than earth.

Through any sickness, health, and pain,
Remember,"For me, to live is Christ and to die is gain."

(Philippians 1:21 NKJV.)

MIN KEITH FEENEY SR. 2/14/1947 3/14/2016   REV FRANCÉS MALLADEW BROWN 5/29/1945 6/7/2014   LOUISE THOMPSON-BLANKS 4/17/1920 7/10/2005   EDWARD L. THOMPSON SR. 6/22/1941 10/21/2010   LUGEAN THOMPSON 9/19/1944 7/2/2012

Stairway-to-Heaven

Printed in the United States
by Baker & Taylor Publisher Services